AF325820

TO THOSE WHO SPEAK
TO US LIKE CHILDREN

Madeleine Melquiond

TO THOSE WHO SPEAK TO US LIKE CHILDREN

A Journey into "Septuagenia"

Max Milo

Max Milo, Paris, 2024
www.maxmilo.com
ISBN : 978-2-31501-980-9

Foreword:
Old Age: A Brutal Metamorphosis

"Where's the old lady?" The man, about 35, tall, beefy, entered the café like a raging bull. He's a regular at the counter. He didn't see me, because I was hidden by a pillar.

It was so brutal that all the customers took a nosedive in their drinks.

He's looking, he sees me.

He sits down across from me. Then he says, *"You're the one who hit my car coming out of your companion's house last night."*

Indeed, in these Covid times, I had preferred to leave my friend's apartment and go home at night because I was less likely to be stopped by the police for not filling in the required form. And with good reason! The list of "valid" reasons for traveling did not include a visit to a non-cohabiting lover. A serious omission!

But I knew I hadn't hit any cars when I left the parking lot.

And here is this vulgar man telling me, without preamble:

– If you give me a couple of thousand euros, we can work something out. But I need it and I need it fast. You're old, you'll have the police on your back if I go to the gendarmerie, whereas if you give me 2,000 euros, you'll be in the clear.

He brings his chest forward, staring at me, his gaze provocative.

– Come on, you're old and I know you have money.

I'm humiliated in front of all the customers, taken aback by these remarks. I refuse and affirm that I haven't hit any vehicle.

– Come on, lady, you know it's you. You can't lie at your age. It made a racket that woke up the whole residence. You don't have the strength to oppose a complaint, so accept it. 2,000 euros is nothing to you.

It's so cheeky, impolite and untrue that I'm speechless, before pulling myself together to tell him I won't do anything about it.

He insists, leans in, his gaze threatening. I retort:

– File a complaint if you want, my car didn't give, so didn't receive, any shock, the gendarmes will see that.

Very upset, he gets agitated:

– You've got some nerve! You know very well what happened. I've got witnesses.

It addresses other customers:

– Did you see that vioque? She's as much a liar as she is rich…

The man I'd spent part of the night with arrived. We had an appointment. The ogre stopped howling and lowered his voice. My friend asked him why he was so angry.

– Oh nothing, he says, sounding sweet. I was just trying to reach a compromise with Madame, because she rear-ended me yesterday coming out of your place and I don't have insurance.

– No insurance?

– What? There are plenty of people who drive without insurance because of the price. Didn't you know? And petrol too! Haven't you heard of the yellow vests? The old lady, I understand, she doesn't know much about cars, she can't see very well. But you?!

When he gets angry, my friend, it's a cold anger, he has a bass voice and articulates every word well:

– You're going to get out of here. Madame didn't hit anything. If you like, I'll go to the police station and tell them what really happened...

The man stands up.

– Boy, is your girlfriend lucky.

He capitulates, but wants to come out on top:

– By the way, where did you find her? In a nursing home?

This is how a 72-year-old lady was treated in the days of the first confinement. In this story, there's the whole range of treatment reserved for septuagenarians: intimidation, lies, threats, scams and the tone of a man lecturing a kid who's done something stupid.

Notice, by the way, that he immediately lowered his flag in front of a man. It's women we're nagging.

What's more, I didn't (and still don't) fit the profile of an old woman. I have a glib tongue, I'm not shy, no man has ever hurt me, I'm not afraid...

This story also reveals that from a certain age, and especially from 70 onwards, we—women—are no longer considered as singular individuals, but as an "old lady", all alike or more or less.

We're all given the same labels: fragile, shy, easy to con, threaten, swindle. An old lady? She's a little mouse who's sure to take a bite out of the trapdoor.

We're also said to be diminutive, invalid, forgetful, bitter or cantankerous, which also applies to old gentlemen, but with more caution.

In fairy tales, old women are called witches, poisoners or "ogresses". This is also the case for women accused of killing their companions.

In real life, our interlocutors can, depending on their position, be compassionate, protective, infantilizing or abusive, contemptuous and threatening.

This robotization, this "all the same", implies that we have no past. In the "old" family, there are no roots, no history, no knowledge, no trials, no experiences, no joys, in short... everything in our lives that has produced this result: an old man or woman who has digested and filtered his or her life up to his or her current age, and made choices in relation to his or her past.

Very few books, articles or websites take this approach. Most are catalogs of standard prescriptions designed to help us age well.

Like tomatoes, we're grown out of the ground. According to sociologist Christian Boltanski, the making of the old is "*the work of grouping, inclusion and exclusion, of which it is the product... by analyzing the social work of definition and delimitation that accompanied the formation of the group and contributed, by objectifying*

it, to making it be in the mode of that which goes without saying".
The ideology of aging well ignores the question of time.

As I wrote in my book *You Can't Be Serious When You're 60*, this vision is already being felt in our sixties. At that point, aging well is already governed by standardized lists: walk for an hour a day, do voluntary work, go to a gentle gymnastics class, maintain social ties, help children and grandchildren.

From the age of 60 to 70, I was on the slope of old age, but it's quite gentle, it doesn't shake us to the core, especially if we follow the advice of the list-makers. Or if we ignore it, for that matter. In that case, we're eccentric, gossipy and off-putting.

At the age of 70, a chaotic, disconcerting and unsettling landscape has suddenly opened up before me, requiring me to learn, behave and take care of things that are foreign to my past and that I'm afraid of.

So, for example, illnesses that aren't necessarily new, but are more demanding, social life where we don't often encounter real affection, administrative procedures that make the computer a bête noire, and the iPhone a facetious imp.

Difficult moments are more frequent than before: tiredness, drowsiness, pain, falls, discouragement, less concentration, less responsiveness.

As things get worse, often in fits and starts, I need help. Politicians have understood this, because there's a huge reservoir of profit to be made: drugs, prostheses, blood tests, imaging, rehabilitation, specialist consultations. I'm part of a promising "market"...

Rare moments! If we are given a compliment, it will always be in reference to youth: "*This septuagenarian takes us back with talent to the days of her youth*". Or: "*An elderly writer who retains the ardor of her younger years*", "*Despite her age, this singer thrills us*", etc.

Youth has become the gold standard of talent and success. All the more so in the case of a woman, when an old man is more readily conceded to have experience.

It's easy to become addicted, to follow the flow in silence. That's why, in this book, I've recounted my often comical attempts to resist, focusing on the women I inevitably know best. And I've given myself the pleasure of talking about happy moments, charming surprises and even love at first sight. As Simone de Beauvoir wrote: "*Old age is the second sex of the third age*".

PART 1

I'S ANOTHER

1– CHAOS

Around the age of 70, I experienced a radical change. As I descended the arid but still mild slope of my sixties, I came to a door that creaked open, and saw that the path of years was now steep, rutted and muddy. Granite boulders had rolled into the desolation. I couldn't see a spring. The only cheerful elements in this terrible landscape were, in the distance, a small clearing of new grass dotted with hornbeam, birch and poplar, and to the east, the foam of rolling waves. It was like a metaphor for primitive chaos, which in Genesis means both wave and void.

For those who dare to say that old age is a "beautiful adventure" and "a spiritual opening", I would reply that it's a ravine of hollows and bumps, of forests destroyed by fire, and that neither eruptions nor earthquakes are spared us...

In France, more people die between the ages of 50 and 70 than later in life. What's more, life expectancy—our leaders and the politicians in their pay are careful not to say so out loud—has been falling since 2010. It has fallen, Covid included, back to its

2014 level. Overall, we're living shorter lives, even if we arrive in "Septuagenia" (I thought it hard to say Septentia) in good shape. Yes, medicine and especially surgery have made spectacular progress. But environmental diseases, epidemics, epizootics and psychiatric ailments are all piling up at the door.

So I was in good health on my birthday, and my purchasing power had remained more or less the same since I turned 50. My life insurance, property assets and pension had contracted a little, but my "nest egg" had remained in its hiding place.

The rhetoric of "we're living longer" or "we're all centenarians" is widely used to create a "demographic mirage" to justify a later retirement age.

Yes, but you might say, there's also the mass of babies who will come along in their time to replace the more hollow classes like ours, the baby-boomers. Nothing is less certain! The fertility rate has fallen sharply. In 2020, the number of births will be 736,000, the lowest level since 1945, a trend confirmed by Covid, contrary to the legend that confined couples have procreated more. It is even said that quarrels have multiplied.

It's no secret that the number of deaths caused by Covid varies from one source to another. Public health figures are entrusted to Inserm, and more precisely to CépiDC (the Centre d'Epidémiologie sur les Causes Médicaux de Décès, which relies on the number of death certificates). We know that there was a fog surrounding this estimate, since during the first phase of the epidemic, deaths in Ehpad, in long-term stays or at home were not published.

According to the Institut national d'études démographiques, the underestimate is around one-third. What demographers call the *"harvest effect"*, i.e. the proportion of co-morbidities, could not be accurately counted in the general panic.

According to Ined, *"it is the people in their seventies who have been most affected by the surplus of deaths"*, if we consider that diseases such as cancer evolve with the decline in vitality after the age of 80.

But researchers of all kinds quickly agreed that 70 should be the mandatory age for vaccination. As a result, we septuagenarians have found ourselves at the center of endless controversy and furious arguments, we've been shunted from screening center to vaccination center, and once vaccinated, we've been asked for a fourth vaccine. It's enough to make you dizzy, especially when the fifth one arrives! To the ordeal of possible imminent death was added the constraint of vaccination. For us, the Covid effect was above all a factor of instability, anxiety and fear.

2– It's in Your Head

When I tell someone my age, they're a little embarrassed. Luckily, popular wisdom has an answer for everything, thanks in particular to the ineradicable "it's all in your head". It would seem, to hear it, that they want to console us.

Do we need consoling? Not necessarily. In "septuagenia", there are happy people. I'm one of them. But we do feel that age has arrived and is often crippling us. There are gradations, and discontinuous ones at that, with "crises" alternating with days when we feel rejuvenated. It's a rare person who can claim without bluffing that they don't feel the effects of age, this one because they have memory lapses, that other because they suffer from recurrent sciatica, another because they're incontinent, or have back pain, ankle pain, knee pain, what have you?

This propensity to say that it's enough to be young "in the head" is in line with the zeitgeist, which assumes that growing old is necessarily a decline. Young wolves don't value old age, we're not respected for our age, we've lost the ability to see all that an older person has accumulated in terms of experience, knowledge and know-how, prudence, acuity of judgment. Long gone are the days when old people were consulted as oracles, except in certain civilizations where this vision has remained alive and well.

These are youthful times. It tells old people to look young. Hence the often-heard response: *"You don't do them"*. Which really means that it would be sad if we did. By "them", I mean the years which, as they increase, diminish a person's value. For the elderly can only be a source of embarrassment and loss of value—in the market sense of the word—hence the view that they should work longer, or at the very least render a non-monetisable service to society by volunteering or taking part in community life.

Old age is unproductive, that's the verdict in liberal societies, which our politicians, the upper echelons of the healthcare profession and those with any power over us are struggling to correct. We should cost less. This is the opinion of many forty-somethings, who claim that the Trente Glorieuses have ensured us a golden retirement. For the past ten or twenty years, this expression has been in vogue in the media, along with *L'âge d'or* to describe those years. However, as the imagery of the bourgeois grandmother dressed in designer clothes and tinkling her gold jewelry rings increasingly false, given the polarization of fortunes, we've had to admit that we're not frolicking in Uncle Scrooge's treasure trove. Commentators and editorialists have therefore gone on a semantic retreat, using the image of *"grey gold"*, which, if I try to interpret it, means that we have a good standard of living, to match the grey of our hair and the greyness of our lives.

If we give the figures a say, the Institut national démogra-phique (Ined) shows that the median standard of living for people aged 65 and over is around 20,000 euros (22,400 in 2019). If we take as a basis people of this age who are single or isolated, we fall to 19,900 euros, a significant difference. Average gross monthly pensions show little downward trend, ranging from + 1.80 euros in 2006 to – 1.3 and + 0.4 in 2020. Nor are there any major upheavals in the "bas de laine", which is made up of 73.4% in life insurance, 80% in savings books and 73.4% in property income.

This fairly stable data opens the door to a double interpreta-tion, reinforced by the Covid drama.

We admit that there are small pensioners and poor retirees for whom a little *benevolence* (novlangue) is essential, through aids and a few inexpensive market services. But if our *added value* no longer exists, the adepts of marketing have sniffed out that we are also consumers. Taking advantage of our deficien-cies, they are constantly discovering new needs for us. Under the paradigm of ageing well, we need a walk-in shower, a stove with an alarm so that we don't leave it on out of distraction, adapted clothing, especially for our feet, which are crying out for soft soles and breathable leather, not to mention the heavy expense of a new single-storey house, or failing that, general renovation, windows, walls and roof, as early as our sixties.

The adage "it's all *in your* head", coupled with the *"you don't make them"* that is supposed to compensate for all these purchases, is in fact a more muted expression of the anguish of those who refuse to face up to their own old age.

It's true that we bear the scars of old age on our skin, our eyesight, our hearing, in our skeleton and various organs, but it's especially frightening because it's the antechamber of death, which many of our modern thinkers seek to circumvent, blur or soften.

We don't need to be comforted with magic formulas and advertising slogans. It is indeed difficult to grow old, and I mean just old, not the guilt-inducing *ageing well.*

During Covid, old people who died were invisible. Apart from a blurred photo of a body encased in a blue plastic bag, and the occasional view of a room where the dead were lined up as if on parade, the media didn't want to dramatize the situation, nor did the politicians or—more surprisingly—the churches. I wondered, and still wonder: where are these missing people, where are their families, where are they buried? Without being voyeuristic, I would have appreciated it if this aspect of the epidemic had not been glossed over, while Covid systematically hid its dead.

Let's add all the reservations due to gaps in the victim count. The press was rightly scandalized by the fact that the initial figures did not include people living in Ehpad, at home or in long-term care. There was no point in counting co-morbidities, as it was impossible to carry out research on bodies that had to be evacuated quickly.

The government's official figures are those of Inserm, or more precisely of CépiDC, which uses death certificates as its criteria, resulting in an underestimate of one-third, according to Ined...

In this statistical jumble, according to Ined, septuagenarians have been "heavily impacted", even more so than octogenarians, because after a certain age, some illnesses don't evolve very much: cancer, for example.

We've sailed into a world of uncertainty, both numerical and medical, which has left us disorientated. In fact, I've met a lot of women my age who've become conspiracy theorists on the theme of *"they're getting rid of us on the sly"*, or who've lost faith in medicine.

For once, although I'm not a fan of commemorations, I feel that a republican and secular tribute to the Covid dead would have been welcome. Governments often organize them for smaller events, such as plane crashes.

3– My L'll Lady

When a plumber works on my siphon, he grumbles: "*Oh, my poor lady, you'll have to be careful! There's hair on it.*"

"*Come on, poor lady, this isn't work! Your tiler's an incompetent. Look, there are already tiles coming loose. The glue, my poor lady, isn't Seccotine, it's real professional glue. Ah, sure, it's more expensive, but with that, you've got at least twenty years' worth.*"

Of course, I'm reassured, because I live in the south-east of Septuagenia, a land that evokes the *Georgics* and whose siphons, on the whole, are not blocked. Feet brush against soft grass, you can sit on it, roll around on it. A tranquil river runs through the middle, rustling and light, like a flute or piccolo. Goats with goatees pick at the leaves, sheep run around in circles.

This countryside is dotted with small villages, and just as many churches, town halls and village halls.

There are many residents in their seventies. They're still often referred to with respect by a word I never hear in Paris or the big cities, "Ancien", whereas it's the accepted term in the local paper where they're highlighted. Of course, the Ancients do exist.

They have clubs, associations and activities, but among themselves, in their foyer-restaurant or at the gym. They occupy these enclosures without really showing off elsewhere. Despite some efforts on the part of the town council and the local newspaper, *"invisibility is combined with segregation"*, to use the words of sociologists and other learned writers (incidentally, I forgot *resilience*, which is also very fashionable).

But there's no stopping the torrent of *My L'll Lady*. Every time I meet a craftsman or a supplier, he multiplies the ma-p'tite-dame not without a certain sadism, for by this he means that everything in my house has to be thrown out, or else, ma pauv' p'tite-dame, there will be very expensive repairs to pay for. And the man of art adds: *"And please note that if I warn you, it's to save you the trouble"*.

The practical use of the expression *"my poor little lady"* is also a test. The painter (the carpenter, the roofer...) can instantly see whether I give credence to what he's saying, or whether I'm indifferent. From there, he'll be able to deduce whether there's reason to be fair or to try to scare me: *"Well then, for these tiles, think about it. I'll send you a quote tomorrow. It's up to you."* The magic interjection allows me to test whether I know the basics of the trade, by throwing out an easy-to-state objection: *"And don't you have any sons to give you a hand?"*, or *"Can't your husband do that?"* That's as good as all the customer files in the world. If you're not a handywoman and you live alone, you're in the category of those for whom he'll do the minimum job for the maximum price.

Many of us know that this simple little *lady* can open the door to a scam, with garage owners being the champions of all categories. So we also have our little tricks: *"Leave me the catalog"*, *"I'll talk to my husband"* (who doesn't exist), *"Maybe my neighbor can give me a hand. Anyway, send me the estimate"*. We're not fools, and sometimes we pretend to be, but it's exhausting. Since I've been in my seventies, it's been a tidal wave. Apart from friends and family, nobody talks to me any other way. I'm no longer me, I've disappeared along with my name.

From now on, I shrivel up like a thing on its way out: *"Well,"* says the baker, *"I can't see the little lady who used to buy croissants. She must be dead."* I move around the city like a frightened survivor, intimidated by this imposing term, which is opposed to me. If I don't, I'm noticed, I'm designated as a grump, I'm poorly served. Of course, I'm not above it... Cruel misunderstandings!

– Well, it's true, says Martine, the butcher said that to please you.

– You bet! He's afraid of losing a customer with all the talk about meat from vegetarians and vegans. Very few *"mi l'll lady"* put you in the privileged circle of aging regulars and loyal customers. It's easy to distinguish this little one that doesn't shrink, as it's almost always accompanied by a smile and a cheerful tone of voice that sometimes enriches into *My sweet little lady*. This *little one has* the sweetness of the diminutives that flourish in the Russian language, showering the pages of their novels with multiple caresses.

Alas, the term "small", used almost mechanically, insinuates that we're not much, that we have no "height", and therefore no presence. We'll end up the size of a baby. It's mostly women who shrink, because the male sex is less mistreated. I've never heard an old man say *"little man"*. It still happens here and there, in some villages: *"A pack of Marlboros, Grandpa, as usual?"*, or *"Here, Old Man, I've put your newspaper aside for you"*, and also *"Grandpa, a Ricard as usual?"*.

With *my l'll lady* and *my poor little lady*, the worst has happened. Neutralization, manifested in French by the impersonal style: *"At this age, this bathtub needs to be removed—it's dangerous!"*, *"Don't cook with gas, there could be an accident"*, *"The little lady may have bronchitis"*, *"She should fix the door, the air goes underneath"*. Certain professions are particularly adept at the *on* and *off*: housekeepers, nurses. At the hospital, we're only spoken to in the third person. Not in the respectful sense due to a monarch, *"Did His Majesty go?"*, but to underline indifference.

"Did she sleep well?", *"Does she want some more soup?"*, *"Did she take her shower?"*. Invisibility is in full swing. We're sometimes reduced to a fragment of ourselves: *"What about that belly, still bloated?"*, *"Does that sciatica hurt a little less?"*, *"What about those feet, still swollen?*

Let's summarize. We are no longer a person, but a bundle of flesh and bone.

4– Consultation

He opens the door to his office. I say *"hello doctor"* and hold out my hand (we're between two Covids). My arm falls back into the void. As if I were invisible, the doctor strides over to his desk, grabs a prescription and a sample of medicine and carries them to a worried young woman in the open doorway. No sooner am I seated than he's back. I hear clicking: he opens his computer on the corner of his table.

Without turning his head towards me, i.e. at an angle, he consults his computer, asking impatiently: *"Carte vitale"*. Then he faces me. I won't say he's looking at me, because his eyes are directed beyond my face... At the back wall? On a memory? On a domestic concern?
I finally caught his eye:
– So, little lady, what brings you here? I see that the parameters of the last analysis are good, even very good for your age.
– Well, Doctor, as far as the biochemistry is concerned—well, the blood test—everything's fine. Except that there are too many white blood cells.

– Leukocytes? Yes, indeed, but it's benign. We'll just keep an eye on it. Is that it?

– Oh no, Doctor. The pudendalgia is increasingly painful, and has spread from the pelvic area to the digestive system. It's so sharp that I spent all day Tuesday in bed, and as my Aunt Annie doesn't live far, she came to visit me and bring me the newspaper and a zucchini from her garden.

I know there's no point in calling 15 for abdomino-pelvic pain, especially when you're over 70. You have colleagues—not you, Doctor—who say it's women's illnesses, simple indigestion, temporary constipation, the sympathetic system malfunctioning, or even stress, because at our age...

He cuts me off. I see the sharpness of his blue eyes indicating severity:

– Madame, I heard you. You've been talking for ten minutes. And you were five minutes late. You keep telling me the same thing. It's obvious that your pudendalgia will persist from now on, so don't make any unnecessary gestures. I have 27 people behind you in the waiting room. Which is your request: your pudendalgia or your intestines?

– That's precisely why I came: pelvis or intestines?

– But how should I know? Do you walk for an hour a day? Have you banned sugar and tobacco? Do you go to the gym, ride an electric bike, go to physiotherapy? You're not telling me anything specific, and what's more, I don't know your Aunt Annie. You want a prescription, don't you? You want to leave with a prescription? At your age, we make mountains out of molehills.

He turns again to his computer, types at full speed, snatches the prescription from the printer and reads it to me: two analgesics (which I've been taking for twenty-five years for pudendalgia), to which he adds "Meteospasmyl" for the bowel and a mild tranquilizer. He again advises me to walk a lot and tells me that, in one or two months' time, if it doesn't get better, we'll have an X-ray. I'm taken aback. I protest. What if it's progressive? I'm then subjected to the ritornello of *"No room"*: *"Tumors evolve slowly after 70"*, *"Would you be operable? We'll see about that later"*, and in the aftermath. *"It will be twenty-five euros."*

I put the tickets down before getting up. *"Goodbye, Madame, follow the treatment well. And please be punctual."* After this word of warning, he leads me off at a brisk pace. *"Next person!"* In the waiting room, it's very hot. I notice congested faces and impatient glances, conversations are muffled: a murmur of mothers cradling their babies, a kid running around, an African in traditional dress with his carved cane. As I brush past the woman to whom the doctor has given a sample, she says: "Is *that all you've got to do? Being late? Don't bother. Anyway, at your age, it's almost the end, whereas I've got four kids to look after and my little one is constantly having reflux."*

Oh, I know and I deplore: the crumbling healthcare system, maternity wards closed in rural areas, hospital "consolidation", scandal-stricken Ehpads, staff shortages, burnout among many carers, maximum workloads for ambulance drivers and firefighters, lack of doctors in rural areas.

4– Consultation

I won't go into how our fellow citizens are seeking recognition for the arduous nature of their work, or how caregivers are resisting this methodical deconstruction. These are social themes that I share, but I wouldn't be doing any good if I repeated them.

In short, an elderly person should not be neglected, misguided or poorly cared for, and, in a kind of soft eugenics, we give priority to the youngest patients, even going so far as to sort out several old people who had the Covid and let the least affected live...

When I left the consultation, I was furious. Ah yes, the pelvis or the intestine? It reminded me of Molière: "*Le poumon! Le poumon!*" for diagnosis and "*La saignée! La saignée!*" as a remedy.

What's most irritating is that, even though sick people of all ages are affected by the ineptitude of our healthcare system, we are considered to be the most dangerous decade. I would certainly like to be wrong, but I fear what is implicit in this attitude: prioritizing according to age, therefore reducing care for the elderly, ceasing to see them as sensitive, informed, cultured human beings.

More and more often, in addition to anti-smoking and walking advice, waiting rooms are adorned with posters reading: "*Any delay will result in the cancellation of the consultation*", "*We can't tolerate any delays given the influx of patients*", "*Dr Soudal is no longer taking patients as referral doctor*".

Only once have I read a warning with a sense of humor, from a physiotherapist. "*For any delay of 10 minutes, bring a packet of nougats to your physiotherapist, for 30 minutes, a bottle of clairette and for 45 minutes, a bouquet of roses. After that, go home.*"

Yes, step by step, we've come to the point where those who have sworn the Hippocratic oath refuse care. For us septuagenarians, this is no small matter. We've already had to listen to a record on the phone that was supposed to make us wait, we've noted the appointment carefully, but a mistake can happen.

And forgetfulness isn't always a sign of flippancy. It can be the result of a weakening memory.

We've taken a cab in a big city because we're shaken up by the bus, we've asked a grumpy newsagent for directions, we've looked in our diary for the floor and code(s), we've walked upstairs (no elevator) only to be told, as we arrive, breathless on the threshold, *"It's too late, Madame."*

5– All Fangs are Out

One day, while waiting in line for the result of a blood test, I saw a man suddenly rise from his seat in the waiting room.

He pointed at me with a vindictive index finger. In a hoarse but loud voice, he roared:

"It's YOU, yes YOU OLD PEOPLE, who are responsible for all this, because you don't respect any instructions, you're retarded sixty-eighters, you're making us all sick and on top of that you don't want to get vaccinated."

As I was there precisely to find out the results of my vaccine, I asked him if he knew that, being over 70, I had submitted to the obligation to have it done, without a second thought, because I couldn't decide whether it was safe or not.

– There you go, eh, *"we don't know"*… but what's this woman who admits she doesn't know anything? It's people like that, who want us to increase their pensions and give them handouts on top of everything else, even though they were born with a golden spoon in their mouth during the Trente Glorieuses.

I tackle the impudent:

– I'll have you know, sir, that I was born on a farm in 1945, in my grandmother's bed in the countryside. The country was devastated, the prisoners had not all returned, there were still ration coupons, and the "recovery" took at least until 1955...

I choke with indignation, but a nurse tells me to shut up, as I seem to be the one who's made a mess of the lab.

That's how cruelty is to the elderly. They look at us the wrong way, *confuse* us, then blame us for the mess.

In front of the elementary school, a group of toddlers tease me, *"Careful, granny, you're going to fall!"*; a woman in a hurry jostles me, spitting, *"It's not possible these old people, they've got nothing to do, they're moving like turtles and blocking the way"*; on the sidewalk, I'm closely shaved by bikes, skateboards and scooters with a *"Push off, you vioque! Would you get tired of that?"* At the supermarket, I take a long time to pay and my fingers go numb. The queue grumbles. In the car, in the countryside, I'm honked at, people give me the finger.

Sometimes they even pretend to help us, only to mock: *"Ah, little lady, you're going to hit the car next to you, so squeeze left and back up slowly."* We laugh on the terrace of the café opposite. It's all the more difficult for me to make my turn as I can feel all these mocking glances on me, I lose my concentration and give up the game, looking for another place: I'll have to turn for a long time, I'll be late for yoga and I'll be teased.

At the counter where I order a mint Perrier, an old alcoholic blows in my face *"you're sexy"*. Maybe this man really wanted to please me?

Like all my compatriots, I'm harassed by telephone platform slaves who, in addition to being a nuisance, have taken to the habit, when they realize that I'm old, of issuing their little admonitions.

The bank: *"Please speak more clearly, please use a shorter sentence, specify the exact purpose of your call".* My car insurance*: "Say what you want".* And, so absurd as to be comical, my hairdresser: *"This message service doesn't take messages".* And then there are the jovial salesmen who offer a product to treat rheumatism, and the long line of scammers of all kinds who target people in their seventies to get money out of them.

My cigar gives me a lot of trouble. I often smoke outside on a bistro terrace. Seeing an elderly lady smoking a cigar is a scandal in itself. *"She must be a lesbian",* some whisper. With that, the anti-smoking crusaders protest that they can't stand the smoke. One evening, I was in a guinguette, where young parents come with their babies. The child isn't even three days old, they take it out and show it off. Why shouldn't they? That's no excuse to give me a verbal thrashing for lighting a cigar outside, not far from a child I hadn't seen: *"There's a six-month-old baby here to whom you're sending your toxic smoke. What are you, irresponsible?"* rants the father, standing up tall.

Except... I have my own little self-defense kit.

First, don't cover the screams with screams so the perverts can't turn the tables on me. This is difficult. As soon as I hear that I'm being implicated, I try to tell myself that it's an exercise in self-control. I often fail, because I'm very impetuous, but

5– All Fangs are Out

sometimes I find the right retort, the one that's too polite to be honest and shuts them up.

In the hit-parade of effective missiles, I put humor, the one that puts the laughter on its side. It's easy when the outraged father keeps his joint hidden under the table, as I saw at the guinguette. Turning your back and pretending not to have heard is still possible, but no less difficult. Anyway, with the cigar in my mouth in front of the quarrelsome dad, I put out the object of the crime, but whisper to him that he shouldn't be smoking a joint with a newborn in his arms. He immediately retreats.

On the phone, hanging up immediately is a very good way of dealing with them, but—beware—they call back. I recently received ten successive voice messages from Orange. As for the usual precautions, I've written them down so as not to be manipulated. I'll spare you the full list, as the tricks of the call centers seem to me to be pretty well foiled by my septuagenarian friends... When it comes to fishing for old fish, many of us have learned to spot the hook.

6– Our Cocoon

To tell you that I value my acre of land, my house with its white shutters, my trees, my flowers and the mass of the limestone cliff in the distance? In my *"Last Recommendations,"* since we can now express our choices, I wrote that I wanted to die in this house, that I refused to be admitted to palliative care, and that I would go as far as assisted suicide if necessary. Everyone tells me I'm going to break down as I get closer to death, but for now, it's clear and unambiguous. My option, which is sometimes described as obstinacy, provokes strong reactions from my friends in their seventies. *"What are you going to do when you're very old in this big shack? It's crazy! Look at the property tax you're paying! One day you won't be driving anymore. How are you going to do your shopping?"*

I admit it. I cling to my landscape like an oyster to its rock. How could I live far from these fields, hedges and flowers, at the foot of the grandiose Vercors peaks? Although I've sometimes imagined an "elsewhere" sung by musicians, painters and poets: Lake Como, Tuscany, Andalusia... I always come back, in reality or in thought, to my home.

I'm disappointed when I see how *Maisons et Jardins, Marie-Claire Maison* or *Idéat* present photos of houses all over the world, "built with local materials" and by "indigenous craftsmen" (I've got to say, they wouldn't dare write that; they say "local craftsmen"). A strange air emanates from the magazine's glossy paper: it depicts a 16-year-old beauty lifting a Berber curtain, iridescing the water feature of a Hindu villa, dispersing a pleasant coolness under an exotic wooden veranda. It's the sweet air of money and neo-colonization. In any case, few septuas can afford this standardized luxury. In fact, I'm out of order.

There are stubborn sedentary people who turn their homes into slums because they don't have the strength to maintain them. I'm inclined to leave them alone.

I know a man my age, a musician who played in the most famous orchestras, until a hand disease prevented him from doing so. He lives in the old farmhouse of his parents and grandparents, which we can safely say has become a dump. Outside, a HS washing machine, cans, scrap metal, rotting boards and tires. In the courtyard, which opens onto a vast porch, there's a caravanserai of basins, pots, broken chairs, pieces of beams and laths, leading to an oven, the back of which you'd better reach with a flashlight, it's so dark in there.

The room where he lives is dirty, furnished with who knows what. You can see a bed that's never been made. That's why I'm afraid the local council will come to *"help"* him, as they keep a register of isolated people. Given his age and cancer, the last thing we should do is put him in a home for the elderly. He has a friend who lives in a room in the house that's still habitable and does him a few favors. But that's enough.

How good I feel when I go to see him, him only a short distance from death, me unaware of the moment, on the terrace covered with green vines and hops, talking about music and drinking mint tea! It's his way of being old, that we leave him for his last days in the cocoon of his childhood.

Some people, at my age, make a well-prepared and successful move. My friends Pierre and Josette used to live in Bordeaux. When they retired, they moved to a village in the Médoc. I think they did it well. Why did they do so well? Because with the money they had saved, these ants bought the village's old pharmacy in their fifties. They devoted part of their spare time to restoring it. I can understand their attachment to this house. It's a real choice, and one they've accepted, despite the shock of leaving Bordeaux.

But I wouldn't have been able to be so reasonable. I couldn't bear to spend my free time with the cement mixer as my companion. Nor that my main expenses depended on this construction site. But they're satisfied. So much the better.

It's been said that our era has seen a surge in the number of people moving to rural areas, especially since Covid. Many septuagenarians have "retreated" to the countryside. Roger and Juliette, who lived in a 5th-right apartment with elevator in the 13th arrondissement of Paris, fell in love with a farmhouse in Burgundy. Roger is 71 years old, says he's in great shape and won't mind being a bricklayer, carpenter or tiler. Juliette has reserved the decoration and garden for herself. Will they be able to live without osteoarthritis, balance problems or sciatica for as long as it takes to make an old barn habitable? I wish them luck with an audacity I can't share.

Have those who age in retirement homes fallen into hell? It's the "topic" of the moment, thanks to revelations about the ORPEA group that have discredited Ehpads, perhaps exaggeratedly so. There have already been some. There will be more. I took my mother there at the age of 79, because of the scandalous failure of a homecare service.

The place is charming, the grounds well-kept, the rooms pleasant, the food good, the residents well-behaved. I neither saw nor "sniffed" any mistreatment. Except during one scorching summer, when the staff, so as not to have to keep an eye on my mother, locked her door, leaving the low window wide open from which she was in danger of falling... I would also sometimes hear, when an orderly was serving us tea, appalling screams, obscene shrieks. They came from the closed wing where the most demented survived... I can't talk about it, because I never set foot there, my mother having preserved enough neurons until her death... Little handicapped and conscious to the end, she would lower her voice a little and whisper to me: *"Here, to be treated well, you have to keep quiet."*

We know what was wrong. It's the lack of staff, the cost-cutting policies of the capitalist groups that manage a large number of Ehpads, and the lack of human warmth, tenderness, humor and caresses—services that are invisible and unpriced, and therefore implicitly proscribed by the establishment's directors.

All procedures were respected, but under the ventilators, seated like bags, sometimes with restraint bands to hold them in place, stood a number of silhouettes, mute or vaguely watching TV, as if disembodied, as already elsewhere. In these homes, there are mainly octogenarians, but also a number of septuagenarians, *"advised"* by their children, or listening to the *"advice"* of their pension fund, or lacking the means for permanent home help. I was able to measure this emotional desert thanks to my dog. I'd let him be stroked by the residents, and one thing leading to another, I'd get people talking.

What's booming today and filling the pages of newspapers, magazines for the elderly and books on ageing well are seniors' villages, often run by the same groups as retirement homes.

These villages are made up of a series of private homes with their own private garden, set in well-fenced grounds with video cameras, all enhanced by a battery of community services: central kitchen, health and dental center, newsstand, tobacconist, sale of the latest books, meeting rooms, fitness classes, yoga, tai chi, whirlpool baths revolving around a figure-eight-shaped pool. Just like in California.

My word, it's like a phalanstery (without work) or one of those communal habitats that followed the Russian Revolution: capital (of the inhabitants) and work (of the carers) united at last! This choice, provided it can be financed, suits some septuagenarians. It's a bit like a 5-star campsite: people get to know each other, invite each other for aperitifs and sign up for "activities". Active, active, active, until the end of life. Those who have enjoyed

Center Park will not be disappointed. What's more, *"it's just us"*...
no youngsters or drug addicts around, no arrogant forty-somethings. Except, as 79-year-old Annie told me: *"Everything
here is artificial. Nothing comes from the heart. Besides, I didn't
realize that it's terribly boring to run into nothing but old people."*

Yes, for many septuas, the move is a source of disappointment.

Some of them are not very wealthy, but they're very clever:
they're couples who live in caravans. Like some of our children,
who are all around 40, these septuas sell their house, buy a
comfortable, well-equipped caravan, and then *cast off*! They go
wherever they want, depending on the weather and their desires,
in France or abroad. If you want to be trendy, live in a caravan!
When your son finally buys an apartment with your help, ask
him, ladies, to give you his caravan for Mother's Day. Alas, I'm
not a nomad.

Wherever I live, I dread the smell of old age. In collective
structures, there's a pungent, stubborn smell everywhere,
like formaldehyde in a funeral parlour, despite the candles.
Everything seems impregnated with this odor, which I would
describe as rancid, dusty and disgusting: walls, floors, bedding
and, as a result, clothes. In private homes or apartments, the
smell is overwhelming, even if the resident is a septuagenarian concerned with her appearance and hygiene. Even with
perfume, old people are old people. It floats, creeps, whispers
death, death, death. And there are other warning signs, even
if the person is destined to become a centenarian. On the
bedside tables, there are glasses with a teaspoon in them, piles

of medication, prescriptions lying around, post-it notes to keep track of appointments. The bedroom is being "medicalized" at a gentle pace, as is the dining room, with its jumble of files and lists, and the pile of laundry not yet ironed. Even the curtains, when there are any, are impregnated with these scents.

I sometimes went to tea at my mother-in-law's mother's house on Boulevard Montparnasse. The apartment was tastefully decorated, except for the fresh, pleasant scent of flowers or discreet perfumes.

This woman made sure that her apartment evoked life. She also had a saying: *"From the age of 70 onwards, a person shouldn't kiss a child. Ugh, it's disgusting to put our lips on our withered cheeks, what's more, with white hairs on our chins!"* I loved going there. There was excellent tea, Sprite and galettes bretonnes.

7– The Empty Room

With the help of an architect, she built a single-storey house with a small garden and swimming pool. Neither too big nor too small, like Mama Bear's armchair, if you remember. She's a reasonable woman who weighs up the pros and cons and inevitably arrives in the middle.

The facade features a standard white rendering, embellished by a bold "wooden structure" that forms the central body. As you enter, you take off your shoes, lined up neatly on a green plastic mat. She lends you slippers, but insists that you don't wear socks, because statistics show that at our age, falls are on the increase.

Inside, there's a water-green open-plan kitchen, "because green rests". To the right are two bedrooms, his and another with bunk beds.

In the center, the living room: a large leather sofa, rescued from the old, "decayed", albeit "charming" apartment she used to occupy in Nancy... I catch nostalgia and a hint of sadness in this "charming". The sofa is complemented by two armchairs of a style impossible to date, let's say bought at *Interior's*, *"because,"* she tells me, *"I'd had enough of all my mother's Empire furniture and antique wardrobes."* All she kept was a small desk that serves as her computer/telephone hub and a pedestal table with a bulging belly, no doubt a copy of the Directoire style. The back wall is entirely taken up by a white wooden bookcase. The whole is enhanced by a large antique rug (rescued from Nancy, I presume). Here, she deliberately keeps things cluttered, with a jumble of books, balls of wool and knitwear, a mail-order catalog, a newspaper with a crossword puzzle (she calls herself a "bohemian") and... *Télérama.*

Télérama, I'd sniffed it out as soon as I arrived on the doorstep. This magazine is the alpha and omega of a considerable number of my educated contemporaries, their gateway to the world. From these pages, Martine chooses her TV program, usually on Arte, the films she'll suggest to her friends over the phone (*"Télérama le conseille"*), the books she'll buy. It would seem that Télérama is not a magazine for the general public, but for the elderly.

An avid reader, our friend takes part in a reading circle. What do you expect, with a CAPES in French? She usually wins the prize in our town's annual spelling bee, and the basket of local produce that goes with it.

She never fails to say, *"Ah, my books, they're a mess. Since I moved here, I haven't found the time to organize my books in the library...",* and I see a shadow in her eyes.

There are two bathrooms. "Luxurious choice", I say to myself. One has a bathtub with all kinds of jets in the walls; it's a tub that activates circulation, tones muscles or brings serenity, where flower petals or crystals are thrown in. And the second? The second features a walk-in shower to *"anticipate"* any possible engine trouble, which for the moment is unnecessary, as this is a woman with her feet firmly on the ground. Just a dull ache in her right leg, as she broke her fibula hiking at 67 and can still feel it, some evenings, some moons...

No technical innovation is lacking in this house. Heating? An underfloor heating system that we don't turn up all the way, as it's complemented, at the hinge between the kitchen and living areas, by a black cast-iron stove, for the eco-friendly touch. My friend exclaims: *"Damn, I'm going to have to have a stere of wood delivered! In any case, it's only a supplement."*

The charm seems to be broken by the weight of the logs, the ashes on the floor and the insistent smoke. Behind the kitchen is an impressive technical area: washing machine, tumble dryer, ironing station with huge steam iron, various pipes from the boiler room, water shut-off valve, electrical panel.

"I don't have any of that stuff," I say to myself, *"but I do have a washing machine that's just turned 37, and a top-of-the-range iron and ironing board. I'm not up to date at all."* In fact, I'm resistant to all the things you have to consider and pay for in order to age well. It's a rather ridiculous point of honor, I admit.

Above all, I feel that something is missing in this house. It looks like a show home, like those presented by real estate developers, furnished and decorated to look its best.

Little by little, I learned that my friend had built her house for her comfort, of course, but also imagining boisterous grandchildren nestling in the bunk beds, or playing in the big bathtub (while she would use the walk-in shower). Hence the double bathroom, hence the bunk beds. And I also realized that putting away her bookcase would mean taking over the house, a weight still too heavy for her. When I leave her, the door closes on disappointed desires, lost hopes. She sits on the sofa, sighs, sometimes cries. Then she goes to the evening page of *Télérama*.

PART 2

THE FACTORY OF THE OLD

8– Metaphysical Panic

"My bag, where's my bag?" These are moments when everything collapses, when objects slip out of your hands, when, dazed, you change seats every five minutes because you don't know what to do, when you make pointless phone calls, write messages as empty as you are, when you replay over and over what you should be doing and aren't, when the sight of your garden gives you no pleasure at all, when you nod as if drowsy, then get up suddenly, walking aimlessly with a dry throat, when you can't focus your attention, when you're overcome by a fear without cause, a panic like a giant wave rolling towards you, a panic of everything that is you, that shakes you, carries you away, in which you roll, suffocating.

Until now, I hadn't experienced this fear. Between the ages of 60 and 70, I sometimes felt like I was floating, a moment out of time that already scared me. But this evening, that little feeling of unease turned into an immense sensation of near-death, a sense of abandonment of the world, when your hands are waving in all directions, your throat is tightening, your legs no longer exist, you're no longer your body, you're no longer you.

I go to drink a glass of water, it flows inside me, so I have an inside, and I splash the water on my face, so I have a face, and suddenly I feel that I have legs, arms and a whole body, I feel better, the fear slowly, slowly ebbs away:

– Dear Madam, what you're describing is a little panic. It's nothing to be afraid of. It happens at a certain age, nothing serious, says the GP, no doubt thinking of something else ("I'd better finish this consultation, which has gone on far too long, for an ordinary panic").

– But Doctor, do you find it commonplace, this feeling of almost dying? Well, there must be an explanation...

He takes it upon himself to answer me:

– I'll take your blood pressure. All right, then. It's normal. Your discomfort may indicate apnea or arrhythmia, vagal malaise or a sudden drop in blood pressure, but if it doesn't last more than a quarter of an hour-twenty minutes-there's nothing to worry about.

– Oh yeah, nothing to worry about?

– Take a little Seresta when you're in this state. It'll calm you down.

Seresta or not, the panic attacks are getting to me, I can't find my cheque book, I forgot my watch at the pool, I haven't finished writing this poem—poetry is the hardest thing, and people are reading less and less of it.

Some days, I'm afraid to do myself any good. I don't know if you've heard of that. I like music... Not streaming, which is a kind of forced listening. I take out a CD. In anticipation, I hear the first notes coming somehow from the depths of my memory, I slip the track into my BOSE, but I can't get it to start, I'm petrified at the idea of hearing the cherished piece that was already echoing in my head.

I stop because I'm afraid it's too beautiful, too moving, whereas most of the time music makes me happy. "Beauty" sometimes provokes extreme emotions that border on pain.

"Where the hell are my car keys?" I shake all my bags one by one in a frenzy, sometimes even crying. And—magic—the keys were already on the dashboard...

As a student and then as a young woman, I was the queen of organization and order: my papers sorted, my parcel ready to take to the post, my shopping list neatly penciled.

Now I buy the paper, I pay, I go out without taking it; I go to the cobbler's, I don't know why; I have a jumble of reminders in my shopping bag, at the back, but no, where then, where?

These are isolated, rather short moments. Soon comes the relief: my bag and keys are there, I've sent my Colissimo, I've remembered a phone call to make. These inconveniences can happen at any age, but what's exhausting after 70 is the increasing number of them and the increasingly short intervals between them.

When an unpleasant mental burden weighs on us, let's be careful not to become a grumpy granny! Temper tantrums and outbursts are more common after 70. When I lecture a skateboarder, a cyclist or a badly parked car, I'm capable of sending them a first-class scolding, just like I do to those young people who block the street and only move aside once they've seen me arrive in my little car.

9– Out of Tune Synapses

"You've made too many attempts with the wrong information," says the voice from SFR. *"You haven't anticipated your appointment enough,"* says a medical secretary. *"Enter the temporary confirmation code on your iPhone. This code is valid until 2:15 p.m., otherwise you'll have to make a new request."*

"Invalid login", "Password revoked".

From morning to night, voices try to entice me: young men, young women, recordings, clones, maybe...

As the saying goes, the children of 2023 were born with an iPhone in their handcuffs, just as we were born with our famous golden spoon in our mouths. Millenium here, millenium there, geek on the left, geek on the right, headphones on the geek who crosses you... All their lives, friendships, loves, schedules, itineraries, clothed and unclothed portraits, quinoa salad recipes, romantic break-ups, spare car parts at knock-down prices, scroll unceasingly under their nimble fingers. *"Farewell, Ophelia, I have a booty call with Agathe."*

There comes a time in life when the individual frantically uses the photo app. It begins in the delivery room and continues to immortalize the first smile, the kiss on the soft cuddly toy, the mouth overflowing with porridge, the first success on the chamber pot and the applause that follows, not to mention the compulsion of selfies showing baby carried tenderly on daddy's shoulder, or sucking on mommy's holy breast.

In middle age, iPhone messages and e-mails are delivered in a functional, precise, self-confident novlanguage, with a hint of hauteur. It's the inevitable train ticket accessory, now digitized. Let's not forget the operational uses (Excel spreadsheets, accounting, work plans) and even less the playful applications that undulate in the soporific flexibility of the TGV. All this is well known, but I'm not going to draw a line in the sand or go off topic.

The real question is: what about me, what about me, what about me? At 78, what do I do with all this hardware?

I get confused, I get stuck, I make mistakes, ten times I start over, I storm. I'd be banging my head against the walls if it weren't for a bit of it, the thirty floors of my residence resounding with my outbursts and sobs.

You object that the same is true of many sexas. True enough. But it's gotten worse in the new decade. Under the pretext of offering us more services, humanist billionaires and altruistic libertarians are modifying their applications, happily adding to them, invalidating one to install another, all at breakneck speed, and I feel like a limp trying to catch a moving train.

My pet peeve is *"bancassurance",* which every day imposes techniques that require three degrees of security. I have to *"enter"* the password and access code, then another security code that "appears" on my mobile. I panic, my right eye on the computer, my left on the iPhone, I exceed the minutes allotted to this postponement, so *bing*, crash, I have to start all over again.

Have I become stupid? Have I lost the ability to *"adapt to change"*, which was largely imposed on me by my managers before I retired? Is my *"reactivity"* at half-mast, my *"sense of anticipation"* on its last legs?

Are these the beginnings of the Alzheimer werewolf? That one's always lurking around somewhere to make us shudder.

My brain feels like it's floating in a calabash. I memorize a procedure on a tutorial and forget it just as quickly. I feel alone in the world, abandoned in front of the machine that's crushing my nervous system, undermining me, laughing at the very difficult diplomas I've obtained in my life.

I open a treatise on gerontology and unfold my brain MRIs. Aside from the fact that the cortex has shrunk a little, I'm still robust in the brain. I have to admit, though, that learning an unfamiliar language is more difficult, not so much because of aptitude as because of an emotion that puts up a wall in front of us, a bit like a kid who *"stalls"* in algebra. Even without the slightest injury, it's our limbic system that panics. The impression of failure, emotion, impatience—fear in a word—are more harmful than the first dysfunctions of the rational brain.

You know that, while always victims and never guilty, women have their little tactics. Not a bad one, the total refusal: *"I've said that when I'm 70, I'll only use a 30-euro cell phone."* This choice is almost untenable for a single person, because there is no alternative. COMPULSORY DEMATERIALIZATION. Example: taxes or bank statements. The tactic of total refusal, transgressive and full of panache, often conceals an ambush accountant, a helpful and discreet son or daughter, or an aid association.

"Pretending" isn't stupid either, but it does require an apprenticeship. It's imperative to have an iPhone with you, to take it ostentatiously out of your bag, to pretend you're reading something that makes you smile or sigh (mimicry is compulsory), and to start tapping away like a pro at something easy, like a text message that says: *"I'm on the train."*

You can also play it safe, even if you know the basics. Asking young people in person at a Paris crossroads where the Montmartre-Galabru theater is located can push back the pocket Satan and open the door to conversation, an all-too-forgotten art.

I was a bit pretentious and wanted to learn. I took private lessons, which reminded me of my childhood math lessons. Today, I know the basics of how to power a computer or an iPhone. But I'm slow... slow. Compared to the nimble fingers of young people, I'm like an old freight train. But I still get to the station.

10– Our Diaries

We've never had so much *"help"*. The most obvious proof, but not the only one, is hidden in our diaries. Let me explain:

For a long time now, I've been buying *Quo Vadis* that tie in with the school year, because for me and many others, September means the start of a new school year. Not just for schools, but also for associations and social activities, and the nostalgia that comes with the end of summer, along with the routine.

I keep my diaries from recent years to compensate for any memory lapses. In truth, they're in a state of disrepair, grouped together in a shoebox at the back of a cupboard. At random, I exhume the one from six years ago (2017).

I'm going through the month of October, the month of my birth:

Monday: computer class at 2 p.m., household help at 3 p.m., 8 p.m. reading aloud class at *La Lucarne des écrivains* bookshop—Darius Milhaud theater, documentary on Arte. Tuesday: 2 p.m. hairdressing (color, blow-dry), take Rac to the vet for 5 p.m., invitation to dinner at Mathilde's. Wednesday morning: market shopping, lecture on film music at *La Lucarne des écrivains*, my local bookshop, at 7 p.m., then *Norma* at the Opéra Bastille. Thursday: 5.30-6.30 p.m. yoga, 7 p.m. Abder. Friday: shopping at Monoprix, Yves Rocher facial at 5:30 p.m., evening at Opéra-Comique (*Gianni Stichi*). Saturday: market, lunch in Nanterre with my son and his partner. Sunday afternoon stroll along the quays to Pantin with Rac, 5 p.m. tea at my next-door neighbor's.

The handwriting is firm, the RVs well noted, with a few scribbles, however, as there are errors in the dates of RVs, postponed to the following week. Events lasting several days are written at the top of the page, connected by horizontal lines. For example, from the 20th to the 24th, opera in Baden-Baden.

The same *Quo Vadis*, ten years later, October 2022.

Monday: 11 a.m. nurse, pill dispenser, 2 p.m. housekeeper. Tuesday: computer class 2 p.m., cervical MRI 5 p.m. Wednesday: physical therapy. Thursday: drop-in at *La Lucarne*, 5 p.m. appointment with neurologist (by cab). Friday: 2:20 p.m. general practitioner, 1 p.m. yoga, go to pharmacy. Saturday: dinner at Armel's (I'm cancelling because I'm so tired). Sunday: 3 p.m. concert on Mezzo live.

See how the number of healthcare appointments is exploding? It's crazy! I spend my life in the arcane world of Doctolib, in the despairingly banal waiting rooms of various specialists, with their ill-posed posters saying *"Become a player in your own health"*, in the quick consultations on the go with the GP's replacement on maternity leave, who refills the prescription and pushes us towards the exit, in the queue at the chemist's behind six customers, in the plastic armchairs of imaging centers where the apprehension of results floats, just as, in the lab, it does for blood tests.

The diary may be explicit, but it doesn't tell the whole story. It casts a discreet veil over my mood swings, late risers, reading lying on the bed, meals with quick recipes, silence in the lonely hours, sudden bursts of tears at the drop of a hat, annoying self-discipline when it comes to medication, giving up concerts.

The *Quo Vadis* brand is a real find: *quo vadis?* is Latin for *"where are you going?"* In the pages of October 2023, the list of appointments is all over the place, and it's hard to prioritize. Lots of erasures and cross-references to another page. As a schoolteacher from the old days would have said: *"Your timetable is like a pig's work!"* Then there are the apologetic phone calls and pious lies, such as pretending to have gone to the cinema to tell a friend that I had a "social life", while I was under the comforter.

The diary is smeared with pens at the end of their useful life, scratches in pencil, exclamation marks to help you remember or capital letters: PRIORITY over the hairdresser's appointment.

You see, we manage. What we're really struggling with is the meandering nature of information that's destined to find its way into the diary or iPhone contacts that we often don't have with us. The itinerary of a piece of information often begins with a pencilled phrase in the margin of a newspaper, the transfer to a post-it note, the stay on a post-it note against the fridge, the flight of the post-it note's contents onto an exhaustive list of "things to do in the week", and finally the entry into the diary.

11– Danse Macabre

In Septuagenia, and sometimes even before, our teeth are a source of worry and need to be looked after. There are the ones that move, the ones that fall out, the ones that have never been replaced, the decayed ones that the dentist can still plug up after several turns of a roulette wheel, the screeching of which annoys the other teeth, the ones that absolutely must be pulled out, sometimes accompanied by gum surgery and the fitting of a post. This operation poses a major dilemma: *"Is it really necessary, given the cost?", "Will it last long?", "Should it be fitted with a crown, in hard plastic, enamel, silver or gold?"* Decisions with the dreaded impact on the wallet.

The gold tooth has long been a kind of ornament for old gentlemen, just like stoutness, a sign of prosperity and authority in certain civilizations. For us, the decision is also linked to the position of the teeth and the width of the smile. Ladies, in general, don't like to be noticed for their gold teeth, which ostensibly signal their loss.

Before the age of 80, a large percentage of the "toothless" (as one statesman took the liberty of referring to them) had to adopt dentures. Half-dentures on the right or left, or full dentures altogether.

This prosthesis has its demands. There's the moment when you have to remove your dentures, wash and disinfect them, and place them in a glass of water beside your bed. When a man (or woman) in the throes of foreplay with a desirable person feels that his dentures are about to fall out, it takes both courage and delicacy. I know a gentleman who does this very well.

Mind you, every problem has its solution, as they say. We need to add more glue, if possible before the ardor of kissing arises, because removing teeth doesn't prevent desire or pleasure.

12– Faded Skins

What I saw that morning was my skin. Not the skin of my face, to which I'd more or less become accustomed, but the skin of my naked body, which I looked at as if I'd never seen it before. Yet I often look at myself in the mirror. My gaze, no doubt selective, usually gauged my figure, to see if I'd put on weight, if my breasts were still high, if my knees weren't submerged in fat, if my ankles remained slim. In short, not whether I was thin, which I didn't want to be, but whether or not I had exceeded my "comfort weight" of between 65 and 70 kilos, and whether I had the right shape to arouse desire.

Why that day? Mystery... I had just turned 76 and was "feeling good about myself" as they say. Except for the skin... The skin. Well, that morning, I realized that my skin had taken a beating. It formed small, regular folds, like ripples on the forearm, under the armpits, on the upper stomach, on the back of the thighs. Below the abdominal belt, on the other hand, it was stretched like a drum over the bulge of the belly. It was as if I were standing in front of another woman, and I was horrified to discover my old woman's body. In truth, I didn't care that much about my body, because I had a friend who raved about my breasts, my buttocks, my legs and my ankles, and although I knew they were exaggerated, I took his compliments at face value.

I understood that the catastrophe was irreversible, that it had occurred despite moisturizing shower products and creams. When you're in your seventies, this shouldn't overwhelm you, but I felt quite a shock.

So I went in for a closer inspection. I saw that my skin bore various scars from the past. There was the scar from my hip prosthesis, but I already knew about it, it was very "discreet" as the surgeon had told me. A haematoma on my left hip, not quite reabsorbed after a tumble down a flight of stairs, was at the stage where it left a yellow trace after having passed through various shades of blue and red.

In short, apart from the little creases, I still had acceptable skin if I excepted the brown spots. The ones on my cheeks and hands had appeared around the age of 60, but I spotted a blooming of new ones. Yes, the rest would have been acceptable if I didn't have so many brown spots, not only on my cheeks and the back of my hands, but also on my décolleté, stomach, the back of my thighs and buttocks. Puzzled, I remembered that my great-grandmother used to call them *"cemetery flowers"*.

I mentioned it to a friend of mine, who smiled and said:

– It's true that you don't see yourself aging. If it's any consolation, I also have stretch marks and pink patches of unknown origin. But I don't have a lover like you. I cover my arms, even in summer. I put on my bathing suit under my dress when I'm in the water and, as soon as I get out, I put on a terry bathrobe.

– Bah! Old skin for old skin, I let it all show, it's still the best way to stay yourself," I said. It wasn't very friendly, I admit.

Let's not forget the martyrdom of Saint Sebastian-style arrows: lightning attacks by mosquitoes, fleas and bedbugs on weakened skin, ants, mites, cruel wasps, cuts from kitchen knives and, if not arrows, whole patches of skin, the playground for mycosis, psoriasis, zonas, burns and itching. Nails turn black, corns reappear as soon as they're removed. We're advised not to scratch. Injured areas are then covered with a fetid zinc or copper ointment and sometimes, as with boils, incisions and dressings are required.

13– The Final Mask

My great-grandmother, who was a gatekeeper in the Ain region, used to say that once you reached a certain age, you shouldn't show your neck. Her dresses and blouses were tailored accordingly.

For special occasions—weddings, invitations from neighbors or family, funerals—she adorned her best black dress with a white lace ruffle fastened with a cameo. Many elderly ladies in this part of the Bugey region did the same. The faces of the old ladies, affectionately known in this region as "naines" for "marraines", were forever fixed on family photos.

My grandmother was right. It's through the neck that death's insidious work on our skin begins, around the age of 50, just like the "crow's feet" at the corner of the eyes, the first folds at the tip of the smile, the sketches on the forehead, the unexcavated lines of the lion's wrinkle... For us septuagenarians, the mass has been said, time has finished digging most of its furrows.

Some women combat this aggression to the skin caused by the passage of time with aesthetic treatments, Botox or collagen injections, laser treatment or even cosmetic surgery. This may be an illusion for a while. What's more, these techniques have made real progress, and we see less distended skin or eyelids. Operations have ceased to be a real adventure fraught with risks, but beware of the mischievous flaws that always reappear! Between the ages of 70 and 80, the furrows become part of our face, and our old-age mask is definitive.

My wrinkles are deep, especially the frown lines on my forehead and those on my lower cheeks. I take them as they are, while toning them down with a BB cream that also covers brown spots.

Men, for their part, it seems to me, tend to consider wrinkles as adding to their charm. Some unrepentant flirts even consider them an asset.

My friend François is convinced: *"My wrinkles? It makes me look like a mature person, on whose shoulders a woman can lean. Ephebes intimidate them, and men in their 40s are too conspicuous in their flirting."* It should be added that men who have been handsome generally consider themselves handsome for eternity. So it's not out of the question to make fun of them by calling them "old handsome".

That said, a chatty beauty care practitioner confided in me on the sly that more men choose the scalpel than you might think.

That's right... I immediately saw photos of Berlusconi pop up in my memory!

Caricaturing a little, I see that male wrinkles are praised and female wrinkles depreciated. See how Moses is adorned with his deep wrinkles, or Poseidon with his cracked forehead! The *"noble old man"* has not yet disappeared from the Western world. It lives on in Middle Eastern and Asian cultures. At least officially.

In Africa, people say "mama" to a lady as soon as she passes 50. In France, emigrants from Africa often address it to me, but with tenderness. I like *"mama"* better than *"p'tite vieille"*. Ask yourself why.

If we take a detour into anthropology, we find that the old man is often a wise man, village chief, guru, god or demigod, or even a hermit adorned with his white beard, while the old women, witches, hags, usurers, poisoners or ogresses have a face like a wrinkled apple and a hooked nose.

In the world of aesthetics, we say that skin loses its radiance. Perhaps it's our gray skin that imposes the comparison with a wrinkled apple, unless it's a nasty reminder of original sin.

Fortunately, wrinkles don't make a face. A look or a smile can transform an elderly person. Wrinkles are skin; the face is a reflection of the soul.

I know women in their 70s, 80s and even 90s, with a light surging behind their wrinkled skin, an amused or affectionate expression in their eyes, a strength of life that doesn't prevent them from being just as contemplative, their faces at rest from which emerge like a third eye, not the optical apparatus, but the inner eye carrying visions, images, plays of color and sounds inaccessible to others.

Whether tanned, disillusioned, twirling like a butterfly, authoritative, benevolent, grumpy or whatever you like, our faces, during the ten years of septuagenia, move very little.

However, my friends are not frozen from head to toe, unlike the "dwarfs" who seem to be mass-produced: the bun on the nape of the neck, the hair puffing up a little on the forehead, the woollen camisole, the long brown skirt, and the blue apron with the ends of the clogs sticking out. I have the feeling that today's septuagenarians aren't such carbon copies. Their faces are more open, they smile more, their bodies are less thick. So let's deduce (or rather bet) that it's not our wrinkles that tell the baker we've crossed the border into the world of the little ladies.

PART 3

THE CARETAKERS' JIG

14– A Never-Ending Parade

In *Le Bourgeois gentilhomme*, Oronte's house is filled with a parade of teachers of dancing, versification, good manners, doctors... Our bourgeois surrounds himself with *coaches* (as we would say today) to become an aristocrat.

At home, it's the *"helpers"* who are in a hurry. This catch-all word refers to all those who *"help"* us: to walk straight, not to trip or fall, not to get our feet stuck in the carpet, not to slump over a curb, to take our medication, to fill in our papers, to use our iPhone...

The *"carer"* may be a nurse, a nurse's aide, a physiotherapist, an osteopath, a masseur, an acupuncturist, a woman dedicated to personal hygiene, a housekeeper and cook, a lady from the France Alzheimer association, as well as children, nephews or nieces, and many others...

It's a hodgepodge of more or less willing volunteers, who may or may not be receiving the RSA, the vast majority of whom are low-paid women or the daughters of old moms (more rarely sons). Various statuses, often precarious, social security coverage and paid vacations only for those affiliated to the CESU. A hundred years ago, they would have been called *"domestic servants"*. So much for that patriarchal term! Once the word is out of the way, politicians can boast that all these people *"have found a job"*. Girls, on the other hand, are often prevented from getting one.

So, as with Mr. Jourdain, it's a procession of people who come to teach us, not how to be aristocrats, but how to *"age well"*.

Ageing well has become, and will continue to become, the mantra for relieving the burden of old age. In my library, in addition to *"how to age well at home"*, I have *"old age or serenity"*, the stainless oxymoron *"ageing without becoming old"*, and tutti quanti, all the formulas, wordplay and paradoxes our creative communicators are capable of coming up with. These acrobats of the word are paid to teach us to take care of ourselves. That's the key word for setting us apart, a tree trunk with no roots, no leaves, no past and no future. But they keep us here, and our children sometimes sit on it like an old bench before it goes to the sawmill.

If, like most people in their seventies, you live at home, you're greeted first thing in the morning by a hustle and bustle of care-givers, sometimes two by mistake. They get you up to make your bed while you dress yourself, if you're still able. Then it's off to the nurse, masseur and so on.

If you've had enough, there's always the comfort of a soul helper. In the past, you've probably consulted a psychologist or psychiatrist. The market is now wide open to "care", as if we didn't know.

All it takes is a trip to the local organic store, doctor's surgery, chemist's or gym to pick up a couple of dozen flyers from these merchants of happiness.

Their role is to teach us how to get over the tough hurdles of our decade, to endure the manias of our other caregivers, to regain strength and vital energy, and from there, now that we have "the time", to marvel, contemplate, meditate.

Behavioral techniques, relaxation, the mediation of a guru (Hindu, Tibetan, Chinese), the Feldenkrais method, the Poyet method, the disappearance of traumas, free dance, the Rosen method, fasciatherapy, and I'm forgetting, will eventually convince us that "we're happy".

If we go to them, you'll find that they have a lot in common with the doctors. For example, we have to be very punctual, as the queue is so long. There will be a few chairs, a Buddha in the corner, a stick of incense, a lamp on the floor on an old, worn-out carpet. Sometimes, they come. They remind me of the directors of conscience of noble ladies, Jesuits, the "Messieurs de Port-Royal" or members of the secular clergy.

Among these new-look housekeepers, you're likely to come across some sort of Attila, the Hun leader who, according to legend, passed where the grass would never grow again. My carers arrive with a jumble of things strewn all over the place: essential oils, teas, infusions, all-purpose plants, homeopathic pills, litanies and mantras, blood pressure monitors, thermometers, an unevenly-kept pillbox, crumpled prescriptions, empty boxes and instructions for use that have fallen to the floor, not to mention the syringe, disinfectant, gauze and mouthwash. No more privacy. The orderly will have moved my beautiful bouquet of sunflowers to put down my paper knickers, my beloved CDs will have been pushed aside and put away haphazardly to clear the space where the nurse uses his stethoscope, where the emergency doctor will put down the box for a cardiac examination ("breathe... blow..."). This profusion should reassure me. Yet a large part of my energy is spent putting everything back in order, pills in the pillbox, prescriptions in their binders, the bouquet of sunflowers in its place, things to be thrown away in the wastepaper baskets, not forgetting to lock up the instruments and potions. Not forgetting to remake my bed, battered by various manipulations, to air it out and dispel the various scents that signal old age.

15– The Return of the Soubrettes

– I gave her a big tip and yet I pay her with CESU. I give 50% of charges, you can imagine!

– Don't worry, Annie. From the age of 75 onwards, expenses drop sharply.

The person in question is the care assistant. My mother says *"la soubrette"* and calls her *"Marie"*.

It is called upon to do everything an elderly person is theoretically (according to a list given at the training course) incapable of doing. Applied mechanically, it contributes to reinforcing incapacity. Between the ages of 70 and 80, some people still make do with an aide-ménagère (novlangue for cleaning lady). In this case, she's in her fifties and goes by the name of Denise.

I have to warn you, because "the helper" can strike you like lightning before you're 80. When family carers are too tired or too impecunious to continue caring for you in addition to their profession, husband and children, burnout is not far off. That's what happened to me when I was looking after my mother.

I had contacted an association that offers these multi-skilled employees (also in novlangue) with the help of the Conseil départemental, which grants a sum of money to the elderly, the APA (Allocation personnalisée d'autonomie) which, according to its brochure, ensures *"carefree old age"*.

Fasten your seatbelts! The helpers come into your home, banging pots and pans together to make soup, starting laundry, patting your pillows, vacuuming the snoring naptime vacuum cleaner, coming to your bedside or armchair to draw up the shopping list. They'll scurry off with your cart and your money or, if you're able to walk, they'll accompany you, giving you their arm—a sign of intimacy that has no place here.

They're usually young women, full of energy and life, with no qualifications and no previous work experience. They sometimes forget to give you change, but bring you lilies of the valley on May 1st, because their hearts are in the right place. Unless they've been forced into a job they don't like.

The auxiliaries are almost 100% women. This is normal, as it's a woman's job. They have undergone rapid training to learn to care for the "loneliness" of the elderly, their "sadness" and their "helplessness". As a result, they spend long periods sitting at the bedside, recounting their young lives and, above all, their romantic disappointments, in order to rest their tired legs "from running around so much".

Their relationship with you is very delicate, because you're not necessarily a good-natured person. And some ladies disapprove of their piercings, tattoos and exposed navels, which don't make them look like soubrettes. These days, forcing you to wear an apron or blouse is tantamount to abuse.

I'm guilty of over-generalization here, because many of these young women are thoughtful, know how to anticipate desires, take the initiative without being intrusive.

My mother fell on the wrong number. Around 75-76, she took a nosedive: memory problems, behavioral problems, transit problems. I couldn't just make a weekly return trip from Paris to Valence by TGV to cope with everything. So I contacted an association. Am I the exception that proves the rule? My mother received very little help. Her carer was quick to vacuum, hung the washing up any way she could, stuffed unironed clothes into the cupboards, but clearly enjoyed the "psychological" side of her job, spending hours "chatting" with her.

She'd taken possession of the premises, turned on the radio, flitted about doing little more than kicking up dust. She'd arrive like a princess, dressed in the latest fashion, permanent eyebrow make-up, false eyelashes, bright red lips, lots of rings and chains. *"That's my freedom"*, she told me one day, when I asked her to limit the fluorescent effects in her make-up and to turn down the sound...

It was at this point that I set about convincing my mother to go to an Ehpad, a proposal she didn't like at all, but which she eventually accepted to avoid the worst.

16– Mechanical Aging

Yes, let's face it: this is the decade in which our "caregivers" and "carers" are equipping us with a variety of external mechanisms, either removable or embedded in our bodies.

It's a gradual learning process, usually culminating in the use of a wheelchair. These inanimate aids are designed to compensate for decalcification, osteoporosis and arthrosis. I'm forgetting, of course.

Adventure often begins with a cane. Holding a cane is, for a septuagenarian, a painful symbol, a bit like using a pillbox for a sexagenarian.

It wasn't always so. How many old people have I seen leaning confidently, even proudly, on their cane? The peasant's or the shepherd's, like a stick emerging from the tree; the middle-class man's, made of beautiful waxed and engraved wood, protected from contact with the ground by a metal tip, a fetish cane à la Sherlock Holmes.

Today, the coquetry of the cane no longer exists. Canes are metal rods terminated by a horizontal bent piece to rest the hands and wrist. The cane has become a symbol of our sagging skeleton. How ugly, this signature of old age!

I don't have a cane, but someone tried to smuggle me something even more horrifying: the walker.

I'll tell you how. At the end of last winter, I went into a Chinese store during preparations for their New Year. I saw, hanging from the ceiling by a thread, a well-padded cloth fish with bright scales. I reach up to grab it, and...

I tumble headlong down a steep staircase leading to the store-rooms, opening onto the store without any barrier. Distraught, the staff comfort me, bring me water and offer me a chair, before helping me back up with a thousand thoughtful gestures.

I'm not hurt, but I'm very bruised, having banged my head all over the narrow steps. The boss is more than gallant: he offers me his big car to drive me home, and gives me the fish as a gift. Half an hour later, he courteously checks up on me. I then realize that—while I'm afraid of being wrong—this exaggerated attention means that he's scared to death that I'm going to press charges!

As a matter of conscience, I go for a check-up to see if my concussion is too serious. I have a slight limp. Seriously, the GP! He writes me a prescription for... a walker.

This devil's device is handy. It's got a little net for groceries. Or even a little metal basket that makes it look like a shopping cart. But, be sure to observe a human being in this crew...

A person walking with this machine is usually stooped, as he or she presses hard on the top bar. Using this facility, they move their legs sparingly, dragging their feet.

Of course, if someone has difficulty walking, the walker opens the door to the house, the elevator, the city, let's say life! But the ergonomist should take another look, because it's an aid that makes our bones crumble even more.

When a part of ourselves seems to be detached from us and becomes a cocoon of new suffering, we turn to prosthetics.

I anticipated this when I felt that my left hip was responding poorly to my walking. The pads that protect the bones were becoming spongy.

I spent almost an entire summer unable to walk because of the pain and loss of mobility.

At the time, many specialists advocated operating as late as possible. They suggested serial infiltrations, physical therapy sessions, or "supplementing" us with various drugs. A lot of money was involved in a dubious battle. I want to believe that this scam is becoming less common, because I see 4x4 posters in the middle of Paris extolling the virtues of walking. "Walk, move" is becoming fashionable.

At 56, I had to insist on having the operation, as the specialist thought I was *"too young"*.

And I did well! My left THR (total hip replacement) has enabled me to ride horses again, go hiking, swim in the river, and I'd almost go so far as to say that this prosthesis has turned out to be stronger than the old hip.

I'm now feeling a weakness in my right hip, and I'm determined not to delay fitting a prosthesis. The much-maligned mechanics are often useful.

More painful and more disabling is the knee, which becomes soft. The operation is more delicate and the rehabilitation longer and more arduous. But what can you do with a knee that bends and hurts? I should add that I was one of the first to receive a titanium prosthesis, a very strong metal.

Our bodies are gradually becoming host to a whole range of hardware: the stent to keep the vena cava open, nails and plates for serious fractures (often in the shoulders), the IUD (but that was before we were 70), the pivots and dentures I've already told you about, the gastric band with disputed results.

In our letterbox, we are invited to a free hearing diagnosis. We crumple up the paper and throw it away.

Because deafness creeps in little by little. You don't realize it at first, and it takes people close to you to tell you that you're talking loudly, or your neighbors to ask you to turn down the music. I've neglected to do tests. I've seen so many people with hearing aids who have tinnitus or hear unwanted noise! I've heard that the system is now perfected and, above all, very discreet. I gave in and did the (free) test. My natural earphones are doing just fine.

The question of mechanical aids therefore needs to be looked at closely. Helping, yes, but creating an artificial support that takes away your retained strength is not useful. Except for the directors of retirement homes who are reluctant to employ a nurse to give a little old lady a hand around the park, and who, at the first sign of weakness or a fall, equip their residents with a wheelchair.

One day when I was visiting my mother, who walked without a cane or crutches, I was surprised to see her in a wheelchair. She kept her eyes downcast, ashamed:

– But Mom, why are you in a wheelchair? Did you fall, are you hurt?

– No. They just said: "*Come on, little lady, you'll feel better in there*".

I'm off to management.

– Why is my mother in a wheelchair?

– It had to come to that. She was giving the staff a lot of work because of her falls.

– Where are the house rules? Ah, I see you need a waiver. Give it to me, I'll sign. Ask one of the orderlies to remove this chair immediately.

The wheelchair seems to be the inescapable culmination of a lifetime, to the point of being depicted on road signs. The equation "septuagenarian = wheelchair" is not quite established, but the time will come...

It's the emblem of the old man. Almost everyone has allowed themselves to be persuaded by the written word, the spoken word, advertising, radio and television: they will walk through the gates of death without using their feet. The expression "feet first" will no longer have any meaning. It's as if, when we were born, an evil fairy had whispered: "*Your fate is sealed: you will die in a wheelchair.*"

17– THE GREAT ORAL EXAM OF THE GRANNIES

The director of the retirement home my 86-year-old mother had just entered called me to *"assist"* her in her *"girage"* (in this story, I'm still in my sixties).

Girage ? What is girage? A bend? A garage?

I questioned her, and a disdainful voice replied:

– Madam, don't you know the AGGIR grid? You registered your mother with us and you don't know the AGGIR grid? That's what we call it, so we don't have to repeat "Autonomie-Gérontologie-groupe ISO-Ressources". If you've decided, with her agreement, that it's time for her to move into a retirement home, it's inevitable.

I try to decode:

– You want my mother to join a discussion group to talk about loss of autonomy, gerontology—which is the science of aging— the ISO group—which certifies related things, ISO 2000 for example—and resources—which can refer to her inner strength or her bank account? So, is giraging a way for staff to better communicate with my mother?

– That's about it. The AGGIR grid classifies a person's loss of autonomy.

– Classify?

– Absolutely. Depending on their response to a test grid, we can classify the person as GIR1, 2, 3 or 4.

– How does my mom, who comes to you for hotel, nursing, medical and psychological services, fit into this grid?

– Let's see, Madame, depending on how your mother is *managed*, she'll get financial help from the departmental council, the APA (already mentioned above), to help you pay the monthly instalments due to us.

I finally understand that even elderly people in difficulty are calibrated to receive this or that sum, which will relieve me of part of the monthly cost of their stay.

I sigh. Again and again, evaluating, grading, classifying to get a bonus: my ability to help my mother.

The assessor is appointed by the Conseil départemental. The director, the home's coordinating doctor and a family member attend the session and may intervene. I don't like the idea of a classification, and one that's associated with a subsidy. But, hey, I'm still going after a three-hour TGV and bus journey.

I introduce myself and enter an office where the director points out the assessor, the coordinating doctor, and in which I see my mother above all, seated on a small chair, wearing her Saint-Laurent suit and Bally shoes, as well as her engagement ring, pearl necklace and gold semainier, essential to her dignity.

I hardly noticed that she'd dressed up, as she was slumped over and as if shrivelled, mute except for a timid hello to me.

The evaluator stood behind a desk, a mess of papers in front of her.

And the girage began:

"As a conscious person, free of dementia, do you, Madam, accept this interrogation?" the director asks. My mother murmurs a "Yes". "I now hand over to the assessor."

This woman, aged around 45, is soberly dressed, apart from a yellow blouse with a big bow.

First question:

– Can you walk up and down stairs without a walker or cane?

She answers yes, of course, eliciting a set of suspicious eyebrows from the lady in the yellow blouse:

– She's 84, after all, she says, addressing us. An age when, according to the grid, serious ambulatory problems are indicated.

Then, turning to my mother, she said:

– All rise. Go around the table. Good. No pain, no tingling?

– No, replies the examinee in a small voice, but I'm very cold and I'd like another blanket.

The evaluator replies that this question is not included in the tests, but that her request will be looked into.

It's revolting to see my mother obey this question at the age of 84, when she still has legs of steel, having cycled 150 km with a heavy suitcase every school holiday between the home of her grandmother, who raised her, and that of her mother, widowed at the age of 24, who worked as a midwife. Later, like many people in the inter-war years, she cycled for errands, walks and appointments. And it was on her bike that she carried supplies to the maquisards.

17– The Great Oral Exam of the Grannies

Sitting next to her, I could see her slender ankles and muscular legs. I felt ashamed for her, having to walk around the table. I almost told the nurse that all we had to do was observe, but I guess the medical profession thinks that an elderly woman has lost the normal use of her legs, because the chart says so.

Next:

– Raise your arms high, do your shoulders hurt?

– No, not at all.

– Pull back harder.

My mother shoots effortlessly. She was captain of her village handball team and did physical culture every morning of her adult life.

I could see her being hunted down like a laboratory mouse.

– I see, continued the yellow knot, that you've had two primary infections followed by pleurisy. Do you have weak lungs?

My mother finally raises her voice:

– Yes, ma'am, and it nearly killed me. I've been to the mountains twice, and ever since I can't stand the slightest draught. At the time, we were afraid of tuberculosis, but I didn't get it. But since then, I'm very fragile, and I get cold in the air-conditioning. So if I could have a blanket…

– I understand, but this illness is a thing of the past now, and for the cover I've given you my answer. Let's move on to the next point.

We entered the cognitive evaluation. A series of simple tests, drawings to recognize animals, or asking you to add an adjective to them. It looked like one of those little exercises you get in kindergarten. My mother, already baffled by the inanity of the questionnaire, would write wrong or forget a date. There were a few simple operations: addition and multiplication. She made a mistake once. She, who had at first taken this evaluation as a sort of parlour game in which she could only shine, began to get agitated. She grumbled. Suddenly, she stood up:

– Madam, I have my higher diploma. I'm educated and cultured. Stop taking me for a little girl.

The evaluator said nothing. I saw her take note: nervousness, impatience, touchy, superiority complex.

She then asked my mother if she wanted to continue. She gave a clear "NO". The assessor turned to me and pointed out that, in that case, my mother would not be tapped and would therefore not receive any APA until the next tapping, a year later. I agreed. The lady grimaced and asked me to sign a release form, the headmistress wore a distressed expression, and the doctor was doing some arrows.

PART 4

THE SHEEP?

18– Honouring the Elderly

Referring to a septuagenarian as "Ancien" with a capital letter is a mark of respect. I hardly ever hear it in Paris, but quite often in the countryside, in small villages where peasant courtesy still prevails.

In the local newspaper, transgenerationalism is in vogue. "*Les Anciens de Sainte-Marie meet les CM2 du collège du Pont*", "*Nos Anciens ont assisté à une conférence sur la vieillesse heureuse*". And let's not forget the therapeutic virtues of animals: "*Residents of the 'L'âge d'or' home were delighted by the little hops of the rabbits in the courtyard, on loan from a local breeder.*"

It's very easy to draw up this list—it could fit in a whole book.

So, the elders exist, they have clubs, associations, activities...

"Old" implies respect, veneration even, and is very often associated with our decade, because 60-somethings used to do everything young people do: hiking, swimming, horseback riding, gentle exercise, yoga, wine tasting, not to mention volunteering. Often adopted as early as the sixties, volunteering is the flagship of the old "active".

When they reach 70, this art of living sometimes endures. If they're not president or vice-president of an association due to increasing fatigue, they find a niche as treasurers, bakers of fruit cakes for buffets, or projectionists of videos on ancient Egypt. Oh no, they don't lack initiative!

I have to confess that I don't much like these structures or activities, because they often (and not always, of course) enclose the residents, even if they claim to be "open". These ghettos annoy me. The elders are not involved in kayaking down the Drôme (which many are still able to do with a young rower), weeding in the library or helping with homework. They're lumped into "gentle gym" or "seniors' yoga" classes, when they could be going to the younger ones and adapting, doing their best. But no, they've allowed themselves to be slipped into the "old people's" cage, a world of recreational activities, with no regard for their aptitudes and everything they could pass on. They are no longer the masters of their own lives, but of decisions taken without them, based on a typical "old man's" scheme.

19– Grayheads Triumphant

From the age of 70 onwards, we all have white or, shall we say, grey hair.

What to do with them? Men often keep them in a crown around their baldness, or leave them to grow out, perhaps thinking that the length would make the bald spot disappear. They're mistaken, however, as their camouflage is quickly detected. Those who fancy themselves artists, musicians or simply seducers, have their white hair curled and bouffanted, like Moses or Neptune. Let's not forget the cohort of total baldness, which is not unique to septuas. It affects men more often, and earlier.

The women? As they approach the shores of the septua decade, many of them have already taken a radical turn, expressing *"naturalness"*, one of the keywords of our fashion and make-up trends. They disdain the artifice of coloring and sport a white mane.

"Most of the time—my hairdresser explains—it's not their natural white, but a bright, shiny white that we use as a color." White is everywhere, especially in magazines, advertisements

and sales catalogs. To encourage people to take out funeral insurance, for example, the image is of a woman in her 70s, smiling beneath her white halo, surrounded by children and grandchildren with hair of various colors. In the background, slightly out of focus, stands a balding grandfather with a benevolent smile. The septuagenarian's hairstyle is simple, usually tapered and layered, a little long at the nape of the neck.

This conspicuous whiteness carries a message: *"Yes, I'm (70… 80), but I assume my age. No need for artifice! My white head means that I'm a realist, at ease with younger people, but without 'youthism,' which doesn't prevent me from being a loving friend to my partner, to whom I bequeath my share as surviving spouse."* Or: *"I'm white, all right, but that doesn't stop me from having a firm and still attractive body."* Or: *"All the same, I go on vacation to Les Sables-d'Olonne with my grandchildren one month a year, and I ride my bike."*

The irrevocable decision is a courageous one. In my book *You Can't Be Serious When You're 60*, I wrote a chapter entitled *"Roux et court"*. At that time, almost all senior women had hair the color of the henna they had used in their youth, and radical cuts: brush hair, a peak at the top of short hair, asymmetrical cuts... Today, they're septuagenarians like me, but the henna/punk style has barely lasted, beaten out by white. All that's left is a small cohort who started henna around May '68 and never left. In this case, it's often a libertarian or feminist statement.

I also noticed the beginnings, perhaps, of a new trend: septuas sporting a gray bun at the nape of their necks, like our grandmothers. Perhaps the new avant-garde?

As for me, I've done my original, which rarely happened to me before the age of 70, because I used to limit myself to reviving my natural blond. Today, I've adopted a deep blond with a thick black streak. This transgressive attitude undoubtedly fills an old trauma.

20– The Black Hair of Yesteryear

I'm looking at photos of peasants, my family. The sixty-somethings are dressed in black, their only leather bags on their arms, their only patent shoes on their feet and their irremovable sleepers for jewelry. In these shots, they all look the same, without make-up, tanned by working in the fields, their buns held back with combs, and they hardly smile at all, perhaps because of the solemnity of the photo shoot.

It was at menopause that women began to dress definitively in black, with a shorter black skirt, and sometimes a white lace camisole, a floppy hat, a black rice-straw hat for ceremonies, and a mantilla for mass. And let's not forget the large number of widows mourning their soldier husbands.

For special occasions, my great-grandmother, a retired gatekeeper, adorned her best black dress with a white lace jabot fastened with a cameo. She lived in a small village in the Bugey region where all the old ladies were called "naines" for "marraines". When I was a child, no one explained this word to me, and I thought it was unfair, because she wasn't very small...

I always saw her in black, but with colored petticoats, sometimes with a striped or flowery pattern.

It was unthinkable that, now infertile, they would indulge in coquetry or seduction. The end of motherhood meant *ipso facto* the end of sexuality. A confusion I recently encountered, despite all the "me-too", among several young girls. The number of old ladies in black was also due to the many widows whose husbands had been killed in action.

Between the two world wars, a period marked by a certain prosperity, especially in the cities, young women discovered the coquetry of light summer dresses, tweed suits in winter, mid-calf skirts and cloche hats. But these coquetries, not to mention the fanciful outfits of the Roaring Twenties, had little effect on the black livery. At work, old women also wore blouses with small flowers on a black background, bought at the fair.

The menopause barrier (in appearance, I mean) cracked after liberation. Women, even those over 40, tried their hand at perms, notches formed with curling irons, Bourgeois cheekstick and the violet sheen of Régé Color in white hair. Long after the Armistice, because of wartime restrictions, they wore wooden-soled clogs, then espadrilles, tennis shoes and sandals in summer, high heels and ankle boots.

Here again, septuagenarians borrowed from the latest trends. My grandmother, a midwife in Châteauneuf de Galaure, north of the Dôme, continued to dress in calf-length skirts, blouses and woollen jackets she had knitted herself, along with a few accessories such as embroidered collars, cloche hats and white net gloves. The ensemble had to be austere and decent.

She used to say to me, *"From the age of 70 onwards, you'll have to be like a gray mouse along a gray wall, you'll have to be invisible."*

21– Messed Up

During the war and up to the 1950s, restrictions and shortages led to a lot of patching, mending and knitting.

The suit made its appearance among gentlemen. Fashions diversified according to social rank, town or country. But these changes had little effect on grandmothers. They dressed in dark colors and kept the gray bun at the nape of their necks, with the exception of the "élégantes" who embraced "Parisian chic".

But Parisian trends were gradually infiltrated by mail-order companies such as *Petit Écho de la Mode* and, above all, *Damart*.

Initially dedicated to the sale of thermolactyl underwear, body shirts with short or long sleeves, straps or chokers, stockings for cold winters, socks, not to mention girdles, the catalog was appreciated by the elderly.

Without seeming to touch it, the Roubaix-based company expanded its range. First, so-called "old ladies' clothes", overalls, robes, thick Pyrenean wool jackets, and a flood of shoes "shaped to the foot", "with flexible soles", "with a slight wedge heel".

Damart was all about comfort and warmth. Its target: women my age.

Gradually, color became bolder, skirts shortened, prints came into vogue, and new textiles appeared.

But not at the expense of quality and virtues suited to people in their seventies and beyond. For example, the "elastic pants" close with a drawstring at the waist to accommodate a thicker body, while the "tunic" covers all curves.

The catalog is getting younger every year. We have other sources such as women's weeklies, monthly magazines for seniors and other catalogs (*Damart, Daxon, Solfin...*). Our clothes are on the way to not discriminating against us, not in relation to young women, but to the herd of "mature women".

If I'm nitpicking, I'll point out that the inevitable tunic-trouser sets leave the cords that fasten them dangling. That some outfits are "coordinated" in a rather repetitive way: the rose embroidered on the right shoulder is reproduced on the left pant leg. The bottom of the pants is decorated with buttons or braid. The blouse is "in the tone" of the skirt, often white or pink, light blue or soft green. A range of "soft" colors.

And there you have it! And I'm sure you have too: black is out, "soft colors" are in. Another way of ensuring invisibility or the beginning of self-assertion?

22– The Lovers

Along the Drôme, near the bandstand, there's a buvette that you cross to go to the cinema. Today, on a bench, I saw two "old people" kissing on the mouth. They were obviously in their seventies, given their wrinkles, Madame's thinness and Monsieur's bun.

The scene moved me, because the same thing is happening to me and my friend. We're not going to hide! It's obvious to me, but not at all, NOT AT ALL to many passers-by and people sitting at the refreshment stand. Most turned their heads away or nudged the person next to them, pointing with their chin.

"C'est' y pas possible à c't'âge," grumbled a man who must have been in his fifties. The woman sitting opposite him added: *"They should be ashamed of themselves, it's disgusting. Do you think they make love?"* The man quipped back, *"In that case, you'll need a pulley to get them into bed, given how overweight they are."*

I refrained from intervening. And yet I'm used to putting in their place all those who make fun of us old people... I practice a form of "pro-old people" activism, just to set the record straight. But this time, I went out of my way to be on time for the cinema.

It reminds me of an evening when I was invited by a young woman and her partner who lived in a cramped two-room apartment in the old town. They'd invited a few friends over and I was along for the ride. We drank, some of us "jointed", and of course we talked about sex, desire and male and female pleasure. One guest, 18-year-old Julie, claimed that the last limit for successful coitus was 60. She claimed that men were starting to lose their virility, and that women weren't getting any younger. After the menopause, they were no longer interested in sex, except for the occasional laborious "fuck".

– You realize, she continued, that Viagra has to be taken half an hour before the act. Talk about waiting for the clock to tick!

– It's been proven, echoes 20-year-old Annie. I read in a health magazine that if Viagra doesn't work, you can also inject it into your penis. And who's going to do the pricking? The vigilant and faithful companion in a black bodysuit and garter belt, because the paper also says that women have to make an effort to be sexy and glamorous.

I couldn't take it anymore and said that at 78 I had frequent sex with a friend, punctuated by fabulous orgasms for me and gratifying ejaculation for him.

– How? says Julie. So you're a case. It's obvious that girls your age no longer have a libido. Men still have desire, but little success.

– Yeah, says Annie, it works on them all their lives and their andropause makes them grumpy and tiresome. I know what I'm talking about, because my dad is becoming unbearable. As for the women, they're very happy to be rid of the drudgery of sex.

"Sex duty" made me jump, but I just remarked, so as not to spoil the evening, that I must be a freak, which made everyone laugh.

It's not that Julie's description is wrong, because septuagenarians often have breakdowns. But I didn't like this way of generalizing, and what's more, by making fun of it.

In his poem from the Bible about the nocturnal union of Booz, an 80-year-old man, with a young woman, Ruth, Victor Hugo evokes an old man's sexuality in a straightforward, but not shameless, manner. Do you remember? "*Ruth dreamed and Booz slept (…)*".

Older people are often discreet so as not to incur outrageous reflections, but I know from reliable sources, namely from the confidences of my friends, that a woman can have desire practically to the end of her life.

Some people do. In the old people's home where my mother spent the rest of her life, I saw on the door of one of the rooms: "privé" ("private"). An orderly told me on the sly that licensed women were performing *a "sexual service"* for old gentlemen, or young men for old ladies, and that the place was also a place for residents to embrace each other. Which goes to show that abuse is not a general phenomenon.

23– Love at First Sight

I fell in love at first sight at the age of 71. I had been abstinent for several years. After my divorce, at the age of 43, I'd had a 29-year-old partner with whom I'd had an affair for fifteen years, one of those "every other weekend" affairs when the kids are with their dad. He was a good guy, affectionate, a lover and loving without excess, with whom I went out a lot to the cinema, the theater or to bistro dances. He had a bookseller's diploma, and we used to lend each other books. Then, by an ordinary effect of routine, we drifted apart.

I wasn't unhappy to be alone. I bought a dog and became a "dog-granny". I took long walks along the banks of the Seine and over the ring road to Pantin. My dog Rac, a Jack Russel I'd found injured at a freeway service station, was cheerful and mischievous, never tired, but stubborn.

Rac and I were aging together. At 65, I retired. Rac and I lived in the Drôme in the summer, and in Paris in the winter, from October to April. It was October. I was walking along the Bassin de la Villette, my usual stroll. I'd let Rac go, which was what the cops were doing at the time, busy chasing drug dealers towards Stalingrad. All along the basin, barges were moored: as many guinguettes, showrooms, organic vegetable vendors, theaters for children.

And then a man walking down the gangway of the *Antipode* barge bumped into me. At that moment, my whole being was filled with desire, and it did the same to him, so that we stood there for a moment looking at each other.

– I've got to call my dog back, I articulated with effort, just to say something.

The dog obeyed and I put him on a leash. The man then said to me:

– Hold on, I'll be right back.

He ran to a yellow van parked along the quay, poked around for a while and came back, all out of breath, with... gold advertising ballpoint pens from the *Buddha Bar*, a trendy Paris venue. He handed me one and stammered, *"It's a gift"*, then grew bold and asked if I was from the neighborhood:

– Yes, I live across the street, on the 23rd floor.

– May I accompany you?

– But... yes.

– We were at the tower gate. He scribbled on a piece of cardboard picked up from the ground with one of his pens.

– Here's my phone number. I'm a press deliveryman and, since the privatization of NMPP, in addition to newspapers, I deliver leaflets and other papers.

He returned to his truck and I watched him drive off, dumbfounded.

I think that if he'd asked me to come up to my place right then and there, an attitude strongly discouraged to women, yes, I think I would have accepted.

It was the next day, after pizza...

He's 65 and we're still dating. I feel as much desire as pleasure, no need for additives like coconut cream or other balms.

I leave him in the spring and meet up with him again in the autumn. He's Tunisian and married, which worries him a little about Islam, but not too much.

24– Would You Like to Dance, Grandma?

Last Saturday, a volunteer-run restaurant in a neighboring village organized a very merry evening. The local council allowed the restaurant to block off part of the central street with long tables. The volunteers covered them with colorful paper tablecloths. Each table was decorated with natural flowers: lots of roses of all shades, sage, hibiscus petals...

The orchestra, set up under a tent, played *maloya*, the favorite musical genre and dance of the Reunion people. The majority of spectators were couples, many between 30 and 40, with small children and babies.

This Saturday, I sensed, first vaguely then clearly, a change...

There were five or six ladies in the vicinity, dressed in unpretentious but well-cut dresses that suited them well. They had adorned themselves with flowers in their buns, rattling bracelets and brightly-colored shawls.

One of them had pricked fresh roses above her ear. I complimented her on it, as I'd noticed her elsewhere, always with a flower stuck in her gray hair.

She thanked me in a cheerful voice.

– I always wear a flower when I go dancing. I'm so used to it that, if I didn't, I'd be like a woman who never goes out without make-up and feels naked without it. At 72, I've stopped wearing make-up to make myself bloom.

She stood there, relaxed, wearing a light dress.

For my part, when I go dancing, I dress simply, but I add a colorful scarf that I sometimes put around my waist, or lay unostentatiously on my shoulders. I often wave it around to amuse the children. As I dance, I hand them one end. The children love it when I twirl them around me, up and down. I often invite young men to dance. No equivocation. They accept without mockery. Rather, I sense a kind of admiration, and sometimes they invite me to dance with them. A mazurka, for example, at a bal musette.

After my conversation with the lady with the rose, I came across an elderly woman with big blue eyes, whose smile made the wrinkles seem to disappear. She saw that I was looking at her, and we chatted:

– I'm 76 years old. I love to dance. I'll bet you do too.

– You guessed it. It's so good to dance, to sway, to do all sorts of improvised steps on a summer's night.

I added:

– Having spent a few months in La Réunion, I often went to these parties, which they call bals la poussière because of the dirt raised by the dancers.

I could see, when the orchestra, after playing the piano, launched us into a strong, cadenced *maloya* to give the signal for the dance, that my two septuas didn't dawdle. They were supple and danced better than many young adults who hesitate for a long time and stomp clumsily. By the third or fourth dance, they're getting bolder, the beer helping, but they dance just with their feet, a little with their shoulders, but with their arms at their sides. They don't dance with their whole body. Then—surprise—a slightly corpulent but graceful lady joined us. She was wearing a long dress and numerous bracelets and necklaces:

– Oh, how well you dance, madame!

– It's true, it's true. I'm 78 years old. I've had plenty of time to learn! she said.

When I saw them, when I spoke to them, I felt a sort of shiver of joy. Oh no, it wasn't like those grannies who sit around all evening calling for help with their joints. By that I mean that some old ladies are really in pain, but others think it's not their age. The dancers I'm talking about had energy and grace. Just a matter of luck? I don't think so. You have to be willing and able not to be ashamed...

Could this be the start of a new way of looking at life after 70?

END

Table of Contents

Best sellers Max Milo Editions

Hitler's banker, Jean-François Bouchard

Confessions of a forger, Éric Piedoie Le Tiec

The Koran and the flesh, Ludovic-Mohamed Zahed

Governing by fake news, Jacques Baud

Governing by chaos, Collectif

A political history of food, Paul Ariès

Mad in U.S.A.: The ravages of the "American model",
Michel Desmurget

Mondial soccer club geopolitics, Kévin Veyssière

Putin: Game master?, Jacques Baud

Treatise on the three impostors: Moses, Jesus, Muhammad,
The Spirit of Spinoza

TV Lobotomy, Michel Desmurget

www.ingramcontent.com/pod-product-compliance
Lightning Source LLC
LaVergne TN
LVHW021610060726
842527LV00015B/3988